A STEPPING-STONE BOOK

WHAT IS SCIENCE?

BY JOHN M. SCOTT

ILLUSTRATED BY JENNIFER PERROTT

Parents' Magazine Press • New York

Library of Congress Cataloging in Publication Data
Scott, John Martin, 1913–
  What is science?
  SUMMARY: Introduces the various branches of science, how they affect everyday life, and the contributions made by famous scientists of the past.
  1. Science—Juvenile literature.   [1. Science]
I. Perrott, Jennifer, illus.   II. Title.
PZ10.S393Wh   500   70-179362
ISBN 0-8193-0539-1(lib. bdg.)

Text Copyright © 1972 by John M. Scott
Pictures Copyright © 1972 by Jennifer Perrott
All rights reserved
Printed in the United States of America

CONTENTS

One	Science In Your Life	5
Two	What Is Science?	14
Three	How Scientists Work	31
Four	What Scientists Don't Know	51
Five	Science and Our Future	55
	Index	63

Chapter One
SCIENCE IN YOUR LIFE

Today the high road to adventure leads into the land of science. The scientist is often thought of as a twentieth-century wizard who gives us such things as vitamin pills, motor bikes, and space ships speeding to the moon.

Scientists give us giant jet airplanes with shiny wings that sweep us 5 miles into the sky, and speed us from New York to San Francisco at 600 miles per hour. Scientists give us radios, TV, motion pictures, gas furnaces, air conditioners, refrigerators, and new ovens that cook cupcakes in 20 seconds!

The scientist looks in wonder at the millions of stars that shine in outer space. Then he looks in greater wonder at the millions of nerve cells that fill the inner space between your ears and make your brain the most amazing computer in the world.

From the time you wake up in the morning and look through the window, until you go back to bed at night, you have all around you things made possible by scientists.

The window you look through is made from sand. In fact, we may say that the peanut butter and jam you might have for breakfast are wrapped in a blanket of sand. Scientists have learned how to heat sand in huge furnaces until the sand turns into liquid glass. The hot glass is forced into molds or containers that shape the glass into jars, dishes, lamps, and TV tubes.

How marvelous it all is. In the magic dance of fire and flame, sand turns smooth as river ice and clear as the summer sky. Shaped into a thick circle of glass for the lens of a telescope, melted sand helps astronomers search the heavens and explore the wonders of the midnight sky.

Each time you lift a glass of water or milk to your lips, you are saying a silent "Thank you" to the men of science who give us the wonderful thing we call glass.

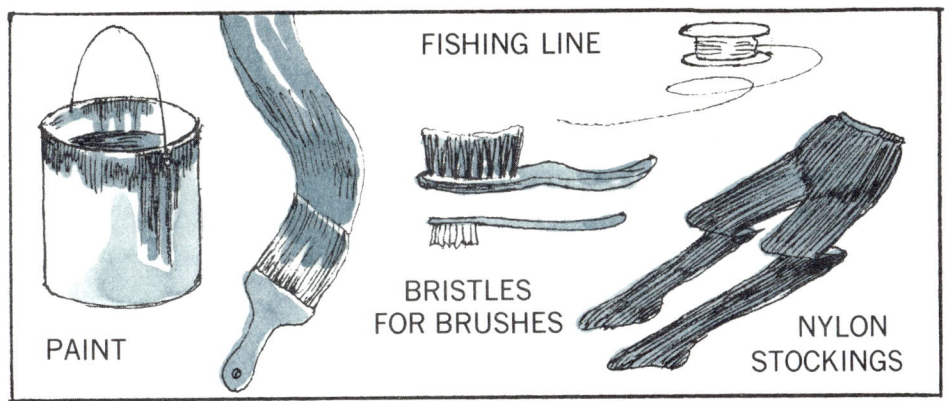

How many things around you have been made, in part at least, from coal?

Through the wonders of science, the chemicals taken from coal are used to help make such things as the plastic wrapper on your loaf of bread, your raincoat, the paint on the wall of your bedroom, medicines, and even the ink on this page. The nylon used for so many of our clothes is made partly from coal.

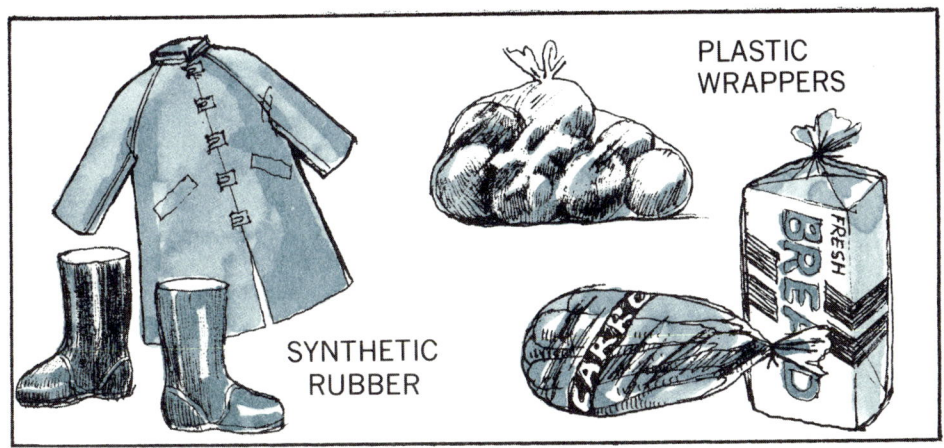

Do you know that science gives you clean water to drink? I never realized, until I traveled around the world, how lucky we have been in the United States. Usually we can go to the faucet, turn on the water, and drink it without fear of becoming sick. In many places in the world the water that comes out of the

faucet is not safe to drink. It must first be boiled to kill deadly germs.

A booklet on water printed by the National Wildlife Federation reminds us, "We haven't always been lucky enough to have safe water for drinking. As recently as when your great-grandfather was a boy, thousands of American boys and girls and grownups, too, died each year from water that carried disease." Unfortunately, the danger of impure water is not entirely a thing of the past. In more and more of our big cities today there is growing alarm and worry about polluted water. Indeed, some of our once beautiful rivers are now called "open sewers."

Did you ever stop to think of the many wonders the science of electricity brings into your daily life?

You turn on your radio, and suddenly your room is filled with the voice of a man singing to you from a stage in Hollywood. You turn the dial on your TV set, and find yourself looking at a baseball game being played 500 miles away.

   If you wish to see how science enters into every day of your life, take paper and pencil, and write down what would happen in your home, and in your city, if there were no electricity for one week.
   People who live in New York City already know from experience what happens when electricity stops. Everything was plunged into total darkness.

The subway trains came to a sudden stop. The subways became black as caves at midnight. Elevators stopped, and people were trapped high up in skyscrapers. People in office buildings found that the hallways and stairs were swallowed up in darkness.

Most people found it too dangerous to walk down dark stairs, and unlit hallways, so they simply stopped where they were, and stayed there all night.

Chapter Two
WHAT IS SCIENCE?

Science starts with curiosity. Curiosity is wanting to know.

Because men were curious about what was beneath the great layer of ice that covers the North Pole, scientists made a submarine with special underwater searchlights.

On August 3, 1958, the *Nautilus* became the first submarine to pass under the North Pole on her history-making voyage under the Polar Ice Cap. As the powerful searchlights of the *Nautilus* swept across

the underside of the 12-foot-thick ice, man had his first look at this strange, cold world at the end of the earth.

Because man wanted to look inside the human body, scientists made powerful x-ray machines that allow doctors to see broken bones, and help dentists find hidden cavities in your teeth.

Men looked up into the midnight skies and wondered what was out there in space, so scientists built the 200-inch glass mirror for the Hale telescope at Palomar Observatory in California. This 200-inch glass mirror can collect 640,000 times as much light as the human eye. Telescopes that use a mirror to collect the light are known as reflecting telescopes.

For centuries man has sailed his ships upon the surface of the oceans, but what was hidden in its depths?

To satisfy their curiosity, scientists fitted up a special kind of submarine, called the *Trieste,* with a sphere, like a ball, attached to the underside. This sphere was the passenger compartment, and had special windows so that man could pry into the secrets of the deep.

Famed scientist Jacques Piccard and a U.S. Navy diver climbed into the passenger compartment of the *Trieste* and took the submarine down to the bottom of the Mariana Trench, the deepest point in any of the world's oceans.

On the floor of the Trench, seven miles below the surface of the Pacific, Mr. Piccard turned on a switch that sent light into this blackness. The date was January 23, 1960.

And what did Mr. Piccard see there, where human eyes had never looked before? A tiny fish swimming

past the porthole. Life! Life even here in this everlasting night time of great pressure and bitter cold.

For centuries man looked up at the golden moon and wondered what it would be like to explore this distant sphere in space.

The answer came at 40 seconds after 3:17 P.M. on Sunday afternoon, July 20, 1969, when the spacecraft called LM 5 – the *Eagle* – landed on the moon.

When men first began to ask questions about the universe in which we live, they called their study *physics*—a word that means the study or science of nature.

Many historians consider physics the oldest of all the sciences. Physics deals with the world of things around us that do not have life: magnetism, electricity, light, and heat—to name but a few.

As time went on, men got new knowledge. Sometimes this new knowledge was given a different name. That's why we have today many branches of this tree of knowledge. Today physics is but one of the many sciences.

It is the custom now to divide the sciences into three main groups, or classes: *Physical Sciences, Life Sciences,* and *Social Sciences.*

PHYSICAL SCIENCES

PHYSICS—deals with such things as magnetism, electricity, light, heat, etc.

CHEMISTRY—studies how things are made up, or put together. Suppose you could take a drop of water and break it up into the smallest pieces, or particles, possible. The tiniest bit of water, or the smallest particle of water, is called a molecule. Scientists tell us that this tiny molecule, which is so small it cannot be seen by the human eye, without a powerful microscope, is made up of still smaller things called atoms. In one molecule of water there are two atoms of a gas called *hydrogen,* and one atom of a gas called *oxygen,* which every human being and animal has to breathe in order to stay alive.

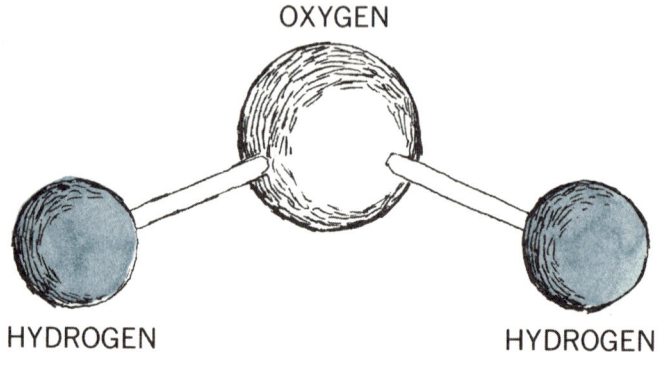

ASTRONOMY—deals with the heavenly bodies: the stars, the planets, and the moon. Astronomy may be said to have gotten its start because of farmers. The early astronomers looked to the heavens in order to mark the seasons, so that planting could be done at the right time.

GEOLOGY—deals with the history of the earth and its life, especially as it is recorded in rocks. The most wonderful place in the United States to study geology is in the Grand Canyon. Like chapters in a book, the rocks tell of centuries long past when dinosaurs walked through deep swamps. The walls of the Grand Canyon are like a Time Machine, or clock, that tells of times when the earth sank under great seas, only to rise again, to be buried again, and to rise again.

LIFE SCIENCES

BIOLOGY—deals with living organisms, or living things. Pasteurized milk is named in honor of Louis Pasteur, who showed us how to make our milk safe to drink by heating it to temperatures that kill disease-producing bacteria.

BOTANY—deals with plants, their life, their make-up, growth, etc.

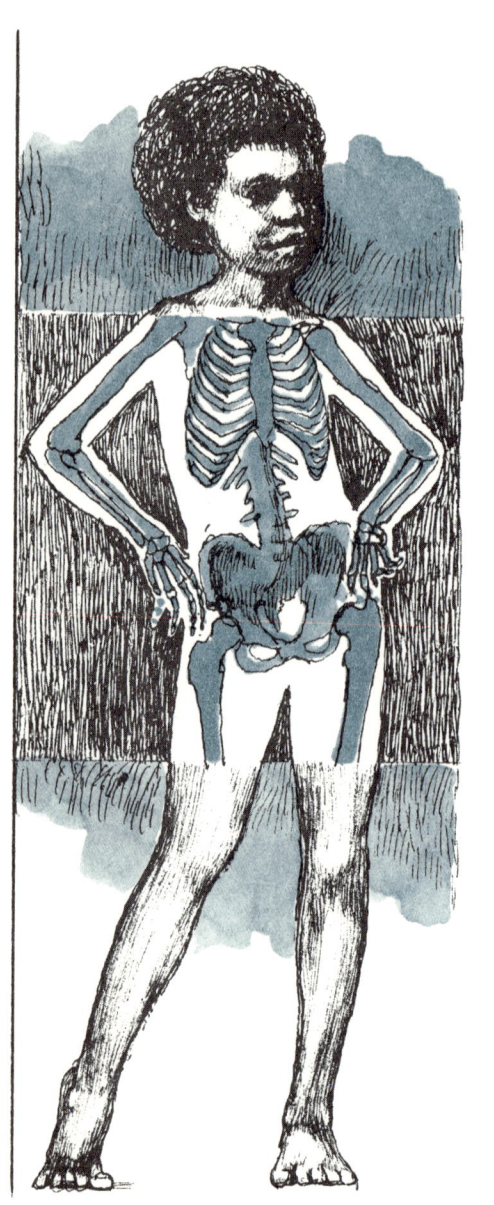

PHYSIOLOGY—the branch of biology that deals with functions, or the work, of the organs during life. In physiology we study how the food we eat is digested in the stomach, then taken into the bloodstream and brought to the cells in our body. In physiology we study also how the brain controls such things as walking and talking. We learn how our lungs take oxygen from the air we breathe, and how this oxygen is then carried by the blood to every cell in our body.

PALEONTOLOGY—the study of fossils, or the remains of animals and plants that lived thousands of years ago. Sometimes the imprint, or mark, of a leaf that grew in a jungle long ago is found in a piece of coal. In our western states, scientists have dug into the earth and found the bones of giant dinosaurs and other strange animals of the long-distant past.

SOCIAL SCIENCES

POLITICAL SCIENCE—the study of the different ways, or methods, of government. Some countries have kings. In the United States we have a president, and a democracy, or government by the people.

SOCIAL SCIENCE—the study of people and how they live together as families, tribes, races, communities, and nations.

ECONOMICS—deals with the laws, or conditions, that control the making, the distribution, and the use of wealth. We say that the economic condition is good when people have jobs and can buy the things they need.

ANTHROPOLOGY—the study of races, or the science of man in regard to phsyical appearance, or looks; origin, or place he came from; and culture, or way of living. The Sioux Indians, for example, had copper-colored skin. They had high cheekbones. They lived on the great plains of the West, and hunted buffalo for both meat and hides.

We have listed only the main headings into which science is divided. Chemistry alone has about 150 sub-branches. The earth sciences, such as geology, have been split and split again, with separate branches to study the oceans and the composition and history of the earth.

It is said that curiosity gives mountain climbers the desire to climb the next ridge, to see over it, to see what is there. Curiosity gives scientists the desire to understand things around them, and themselves, or, at least, to try to find out how things happen.

Part of being a scientist, therefore, comes from wanting to find things out for yourself. You are your own detective interested in tracking down Nature's secrets.

Like any good detective, the scientist also has to have the ability to reason, to think his way through a problem.

A taxicab driver may know the names and locations of all the streets in a city and the best way to get from one point to another. He has a great amount of knowledge, but we do not call this kind of knowledge science.

Science is a body of knowledge based on facts, and organized so as to make it possible to understand why things are as they are, and to solve new problems about these observations. Each kind of science differs from every other in the facts about which it is concerned.

Science, then, is man's way of finding out. It is a body of organized information. It is a method of discovery. It is investigating and drawing conclusions. Experiments are used to get the facts, and to prove what one thought might be true, or to throw it aside if it turns out not to be true.

Chapter Three
HOW SCIENTISTS WORK

Scientists learn about nature by *observation* and *experimentation*. (Observation is looking at, or taking notice; experimentation is making a test, or demonstrating.)

A scientist by the name of Galileo Galilei began one of the most amazing scientific careers in history, while saying his prayers in church!

Twenty-two-year-old Galileo had entered the Cathedral in Pisa in Italy to say his prayers. As Galileo looked toward the altar, he noticed a man lighting a lamp that hung from a long chain, fastened to the high ceiling. As the man left, he accidentally pushed against the lamp, which began to swing. Galileo became fascinated by the back-and-forth motion of the lamp, and timed it with the beating of his pulse. He placed the fingers of his right hand on his left wrist, as he had been taught to do in one of his medical classes.

As Galileo watched the swinging lamp, a strange thing happened. The lamp began to swing through smaller and smaller arcs. (An arc is a curved line.) The distance covered on each swing was less, and yet —and this was the interesting thing—the lamp took as much time to swing through a small arc as through a large one.

Overcome with curiosity, Galileo continued with experiments in his home. Here are some of Galileo's experiments for you to try:

Get a piece of string about three feet long. Tie one end to some fixed support, such as a shower rod, so that it will be free to swing.

On the free end of the string tie a weight, which is called the *bob*. The weight or bob may be anything handy—a key, a nail, a ring, or even an apple with its stem in good shape. The string with the bob tied on the end is called a *pendulum*.

In the figure on the right, B is the bob at rest. Pull the bob to A. Let the bob go, and it will swing from A to C. This distance from A to C is called an arc.

The time needed for the bob to swing from A to

C and back again is called the period of the pendulum.

It is easier to find out how long it takes the bob to make one complete swing, from A to C, and back again to A, if you have help from a friend. The friend will have the job of watching the second hand of a clock or watch.

Pull the bob a small distance to one side in the direction of A. Tell your friend, who is looking at the second hand of a clock, to say "Go" when the second hand is on 1.

When your friend says "Go" you are to let go of the bob. Let the bob swing from A to C and back again to A. When the bob returns to A, say "Stop."

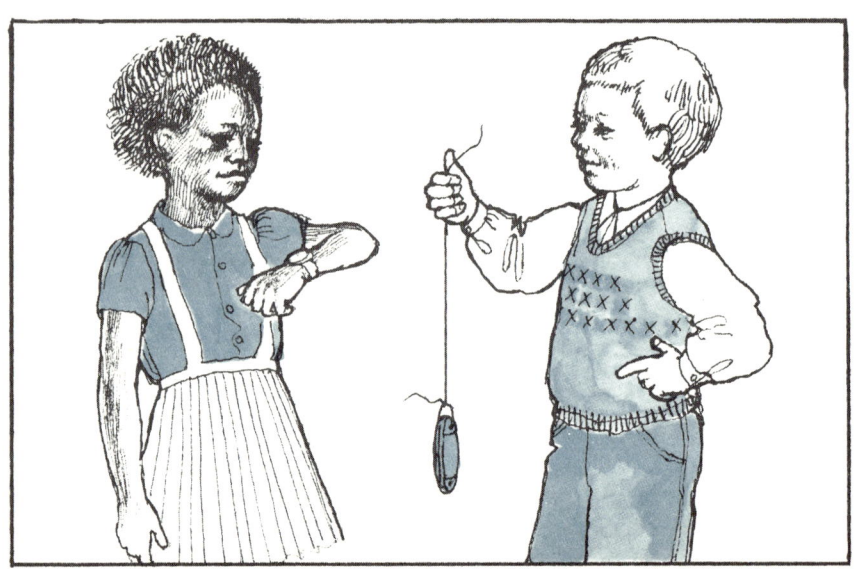

At this moment your friend is to note where the second hand is on the clock. Write down the time it took to make one swing.

Now pull the bob a greater distance to one side in the direction of A and do the same experiment over again. What do you find?

The results will show that it takes as much time for the bob to swing through a big arc (big distance) as it does to swing through a small arc.

Now get another string, and tie a heavier weight to it. Be sure the string on this second pendulum is exactly the same length as that on the first pendulum.

Repeat the same experiment you did with the lighter bob. What do you find?

The results will show that the heavy weight took the same time to make the swings as the light weight did. The time needed to make a complete swing has nothing to do with the weight of the bob.

Another way to prove that the weight of the bob

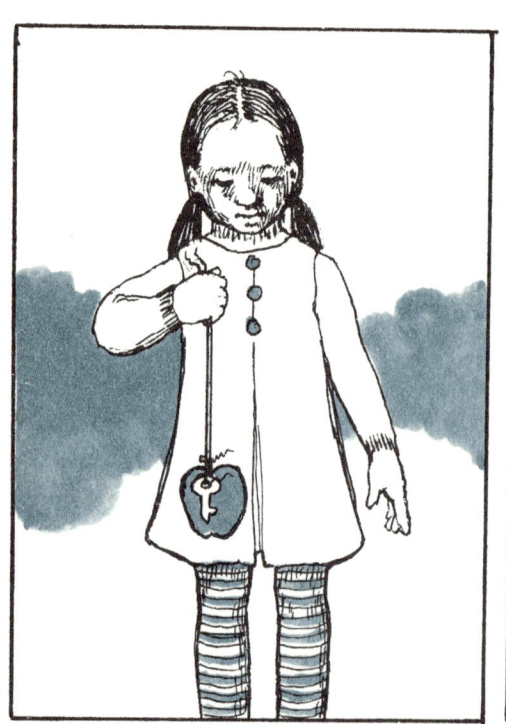

has nothing to do with its speed is to tie two strings alongside each other. Both strings must be the same length, but one will have a light bob, and one a heavy bob. Take both bobs in your hand at the same time and pull them in the same direction to one side. Let both bobs go at the same time. Note what happens. The bobs keep time, swinging back and forth together, even though one is lighter than the other.

Let's try another experiment. This time we will try to find out whether or not the length of the pendulum has anything to do with the time needed to make a swing.

Tie a bob to a string about one or two yards long. (A yard is three feet, or thirty-six inches.) With the aid of your friend, time this swing as you did in the first experiment. Now shorten the string to six inches or less. Again find the time needed for a complete swing.

What do you find?

The results show that the longer the pendulum, the longer the time needed to make a swing.

Another way to prove that the time needed for a pendulum to make a swing depends on its length is to tie a short and long string alongside each other on a support as shown in the picture. Use equal weights for both bobs. Take both bobs in your hand at the same time and pull them in the same direction to one side. Let both bobs go at the same time. Note what happens. The bobs do not keep time. The shorter pendulum swings faster.

Perhaps you will be as amazed as Galileo was to find that the time needed for the pendulum to make a swing back and forth does not depend upon the size of the arc through which it swings. It does not depend on the size or weight of the bob. It depends only on the length of the pendulum.

To further prove that the speed of a falling body does not depend on its weight, Galileo continued with still another experiment, which you, too, can do.

You will need a smooth board or plank about four inches wide and about three feet long. Place one end of the plank on the top of a stack of books, or anything else handy, and let the other end rest on the table. This is called an *inclined plane.*

Now get two round objects of different weights. A big and a small marble will do. Take both marbles and hold them at the top of the inclined plane at position A. Be sure that both marbles are lined up so that they are the same distance from the table.

Let both marbles go at the same time. What do you notice?

Even though the marbles are of different weights, they both reach the table at the same time. Again we find that the weight of a body has no effect on its speed.

The most exciting of Galileo's demonstrations on falling objects was done, according to legend, at the famous Leaning Tower of Pisa. (A legend is a story that may or may not be true.) According to this story, Galileo climbed to the top of the Tower, leaned over the side, and dropped two different weights. Both weights hit the ground at the same time.

If you did the experiments with the pendulum and the marbles, you found out how one scientist went about his work, and you made use of what is called the *scientific method*—the method, or way, to solve problems. Let us go back, now, and trace the steps in this scientific method.

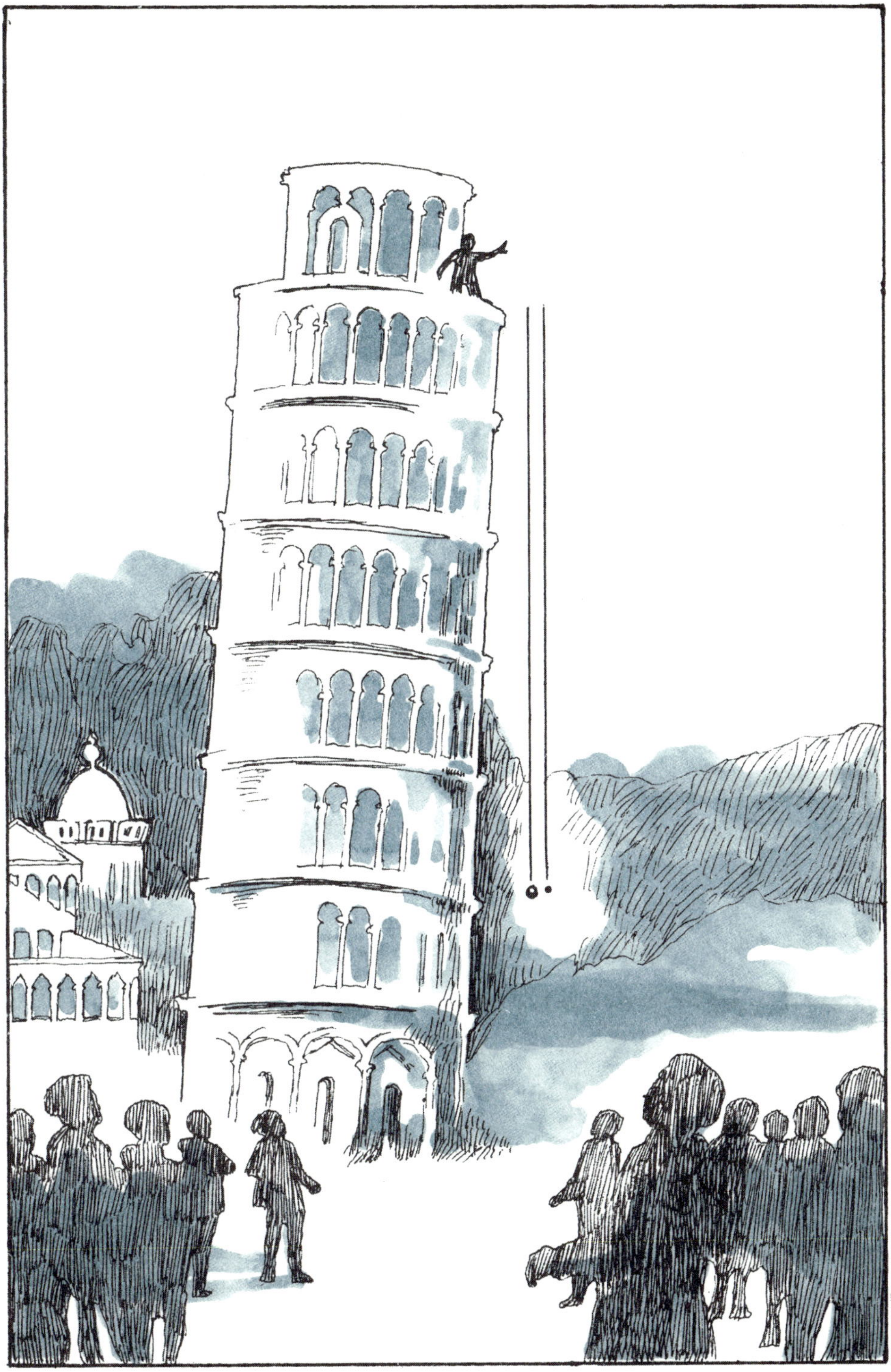

1. First, there was a problem. Galileo wondered, "What does the time needed for a pendulum to make one complete swing depend upon?"

2. He made a number of guesses. Perhaps the time would depend on the arc, or the distance through which the bob swings. Perhaps the weight of the bob would change the time. Perhaps the length of the pendulum would change the time.

3. The next step was to collect data, or facts. This he did by letting the bob swing through both small and big arcs. He used different weights for bobs. He used pendulums of different lengths.

4. The answers, or conclusions, he drew from the data were: the time needed for a pendulum to make one complete swing does not depend on the arc. It does not depend on the weight of the bob. It depends only on the length. In other words, the speed of a falling body (in this case the bob) does not depend on its weight.

5. To be sure that his conclusions were correct,

Galileo repeated his experiments many times, and checked for any mistakes, or errors.

6. As an added proof of the fact that the speed of a falling body does not depend on its weight, Galileo placed heavy and light balls at the top of an inclined plane. He let them go, and found that they reached the bottom at the same time.

Sometimes scientists have to be quite clever to think of an experiment that will prove their point.

Do you know how Joseph Priestley, the eighteenth-century chemist, discovered that plants give out oxygen? (Oxygen is the part of the air you breathe that keeps you alive.)

Joseph Priestley put mice in a sealed jar in which there were plants. The mice lived. When he placed mice in a sealed jar without plants, the mice died.

Sometimes a scientist carries on his experiments only at the risk of death!

At the peril of his own life, Louis Pasteur used a glass tube to suck saliva, or spit, from the foaming mouths of dogs who had the disease known as rabies. Then he injected this saliva into rabbits.

When the rabbits had the disease, he took out the rabbits' spinal cords. This is the main place the deadly rabies poison attacks. Pasteur hung the deadly cords up to dry, hoping this would weaken the virus, or poison, to a point where it would not be deadly any more.

After the cords had been drying for fourteen days, they were ground up and mixed with a liquid. This mixture was injected into animals. Pasteur's hunch was right. The mixture did not give rabies to the research animals.

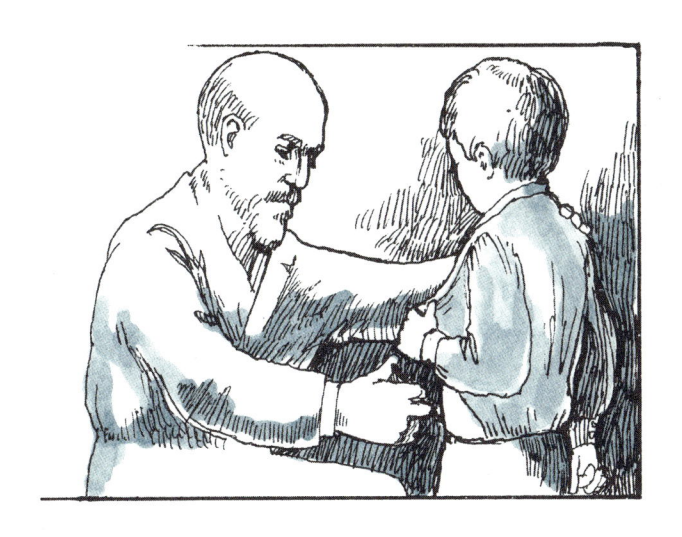

But the big question was not yet answered. Would the mixture, called a *vaccine,* protect human beings?

On July 6, 1885, Pasteur had a terrible opportunity to find the answer.

The thing to remember is that at this time in history rabies was so powerful that no person had ever been heard of who lived after being bitten by an animal that had it.

A nine-year-old boy, Joseph Meister, had been bitten fourteen times by a dog with rabies and Joseph was almost certain to die. Yet Pasteur knew that if he gave the boy his vaccine and it failed, his medical enemies might charge him with murder!

With worry and doubt Pasteur shot vaccine made from the fourteen-day rabbit cord into the sick boy. The boy lived.

The good news spread. Dozens of bitten people crowded into Pasteur's tiny laboratory to be given the vaccine.

By now you see that different scientists discover new things by different methods. Galileo used exact measurements and mathematics to reach his conclusion.

Louis Pasteur had no mathematics to guide him. He had to make a leap in the dark, guided only by his own brilliant mind, and at the risk of his life and reputation.

Some writers of history divide scientists into two groups: the data-gatherers who collect facts, and the theory-makers, who dream the impossible dream. (A theory may be called a guess or a mental plan of the way to do something.)

The larger group of scientists are data-gatherers

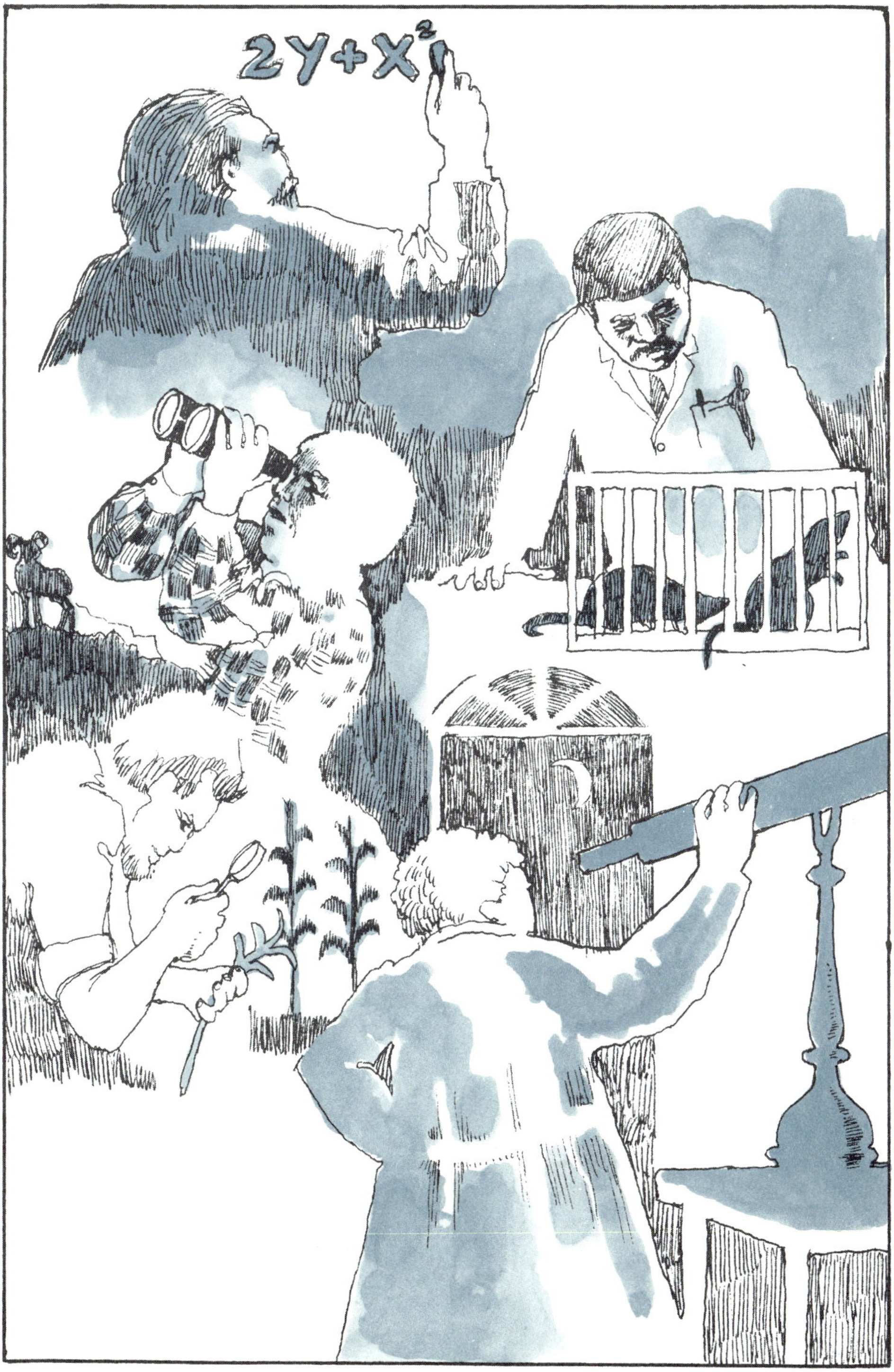
2Y+X2

who follow more or less closely the scientific method.

We became data-gatherers when we followed the scientific method and repeated the experiments that led Galileo to his discoveries.

The second and much smaller group of scientists are the theory-makers, who sometimes may seem like dreamers chasing visions, and spinning ideas out of the blue sky.

One such theory-maker is Dr. Charles Townes, the man who gave us the theory that led to the ruby red laser, the new beam of light so powerful it can punch a hole in a piece of steel, and yet so delicate it can be used in an operation on the human eye.

Charles Townes got the ideas that led to the laser while he was sitting on a park bench, in early spring, in Washington, D.C., looking at some flowers.

Charles Townes tells us that "the great scientific discoveries, the real leaps, do not usually come from the so-called scientific method, but by revelations which are just as real."

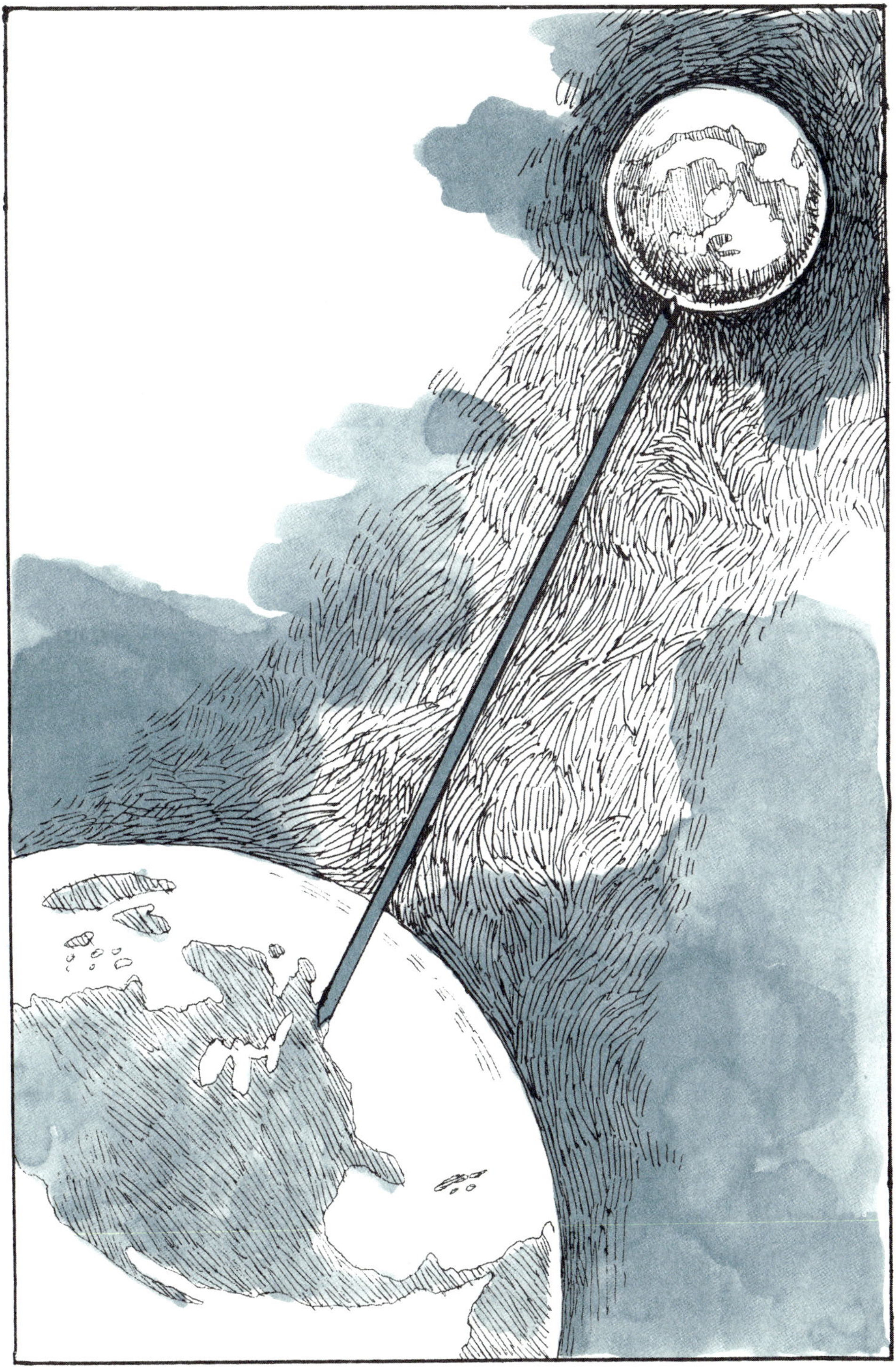

In revelations, we are shown things that were not known before.

Other famous scientists who got many of their ideas by revelations are Sir Isaac Newton and Albert Einstein. Our Apollo flights to the moon depended upon very important laws of physics given to us by Isaac Newton. The theories of Albert Einstein helped make possible the nuclear power plants now making electricity in many parts of the United States.

Chapter Four
WHAT SCIENTISTS DON'T KNOW

Every time we solve one problem in science, it is like opening a door, only to find a long hallway, or corridor, stretching before us, with many more doors on both sides waiting their turn to be opened.

Or, as one scientist put it, "There is now more unknown than known."

Even the rocks brought back from the moon show that none of the theories invented to explain it are able to do the job. The moon, shining up there in the night sky, is a greater mystery than it ever was before.

Among the many mysteries of science, here are but a few: What is magnetism? What is electricity? What is light?

We have already told of the trip Jacques Piccard made into the deepest part of the world's oceans. More recently he made a voyage for one month in the experimental submarine, *Ben Franklin,* in the Gulf Stream, that great "river in the Atlantic Ocean" that flows north from the Gulf of Mexico.

Hundreds of feet below the surface of the Atlantic Ocean the *Ben Franklin,* with six men aboard, drifted silently northward with the flow of the Gulf Stream, from Florida to Massachusetts.

With its engines cut off, the *Ben Franklin* moved with the current without rising to the surface. From viewing windows man got a new look at the mysterious ocean.

After the voyage Mr. Piccard said, "The Gulf Stream has been deeply studied and a few secrets have been uncovered." But he added that it will probably always hide most of its mysteries from man.

According to Mr. Piccard, the more you study science, the more mysteries you find. Like a great ocean, the mysteries seem to stretch out in all directions.

Another scientist reminds us that "There are many questions that seem to be beyond the power of the human mind to answer."

Sir Isaac Newton is thought of as one of the greatest scientists of all times. The world paid him honor for all he did to bring to light new ideas, and to thank him for his work in advancing science. Yet, in spite of his great knowledge, here is what Newton said of himself:

"I do not know what I may appear to the world, but to myself I seem to have been like a boy playing on the seashore... now and then finding a smoother pebble or a prettier shell than ordinary, while the great ocean of truth lay all undiscovered before me."

Chapter Five
SCIENCE AND OUR FUTURE

What is science?

Today, for most of us, science is a way of living. For example, in Chapter One we read about some of the many things science does for us every day. Turn on a switch, and electric light floods our room. Turn on the faucet, and water leaps out of the pipe into our glass.

Tomorrow, however, science may be necessary to keep alive!

Why will science be even more important in the years to come? Some of the experiences of the astronauts may help us to understand.

Astronaut Michael Collins let us share the thoughts that went through his mind as he orbited 70 miles above the surface of the moon: "I thought about the planet, Earth, and what a magnificent place to live it is. I thought about how nice it would be to get back to Planet Earth, and to see blue water for a change instead of this vacuum world that I was going around and around... We're extremely lucky just to have the air to breathe and the ocean to cup in our hands and pour over our heads."

When Astronaut Frank Borman returned to Planet Earth, he said that the view of the earth from the moon should remind us that "We are really riders on the earth together. And we share such a beautiful planet. It's small and beautiful and fragile. The earth expanse itself is very small, a very confining place."

Unfortunately, we have been giving our "small and beautiful and fragile" Planet Earth a hard time.

Smokestacks of factories have been covering the sky with thick clouds of smoke and soot. Cities pour waste materials into rivers and lakes and make the water unfit to "cup in our hands and pour over our heads."

In mid-summer one year, New York City suffered through a long week of air pollution when stale, smoke-filled air was trapped over the city. Millions of people coughed, choked, and struggled through the smog.

Even such places as Phoenix, Arizona, once known for its pure air, and Missoula, Montana, the center of the "big sky" country, have been suffering from polluted air.

In 1970, smog from Los Angeles crept out 83 miles into the San Bernardino National Forest and killed 1,010 acres of giant pine trees.

By now, perhaps, you can see why we will have to call upon science to keep us alive. If we wish to protect our "small and beautiful and fragile" Planet Earth, we will have to call upon scientists for even greater help.

Scientists tell us that the job of cleaning up the world's air and water and soil will be even harder to do than putting a man on the moon. The thing to keep in mind, however, is that it can still be done.

In Anaconda, Montana is the tallest smokestack in our country. It is one of the first places in the United States to use a most successful method of taking particles out of the smoke.

In addition to helping clean up the air, the Anaconda people are also among the first to help clean up the water. Each day thousands of gallons of water are used in the giant Anaconda plant. The waste water, however, is not dumped into the river. It is sent into 700 acres of settling ponds, or man-made lakes, where the water is purified. Only clean water is returned to Clark Fork River. (See picture, page 60.)

For centuries people in London talked about their skies filled with soot that looked like black snowflakes. During the great smog of 1952, which covered London for four days, some 4,000 people were killed by the polluted air. Twice that number died later as a result of those four terrible days.

People went to work to clean up the air. Today, London's air is cleaner than that of almost any other big city in the world. London now gets about twice as many hours of sunshine in the winter as it used to get not many years ago.

The most pleasing result for the London bird watchers is that songbirds, missing from the city for many years, are now returning.

In many other places around the world, people are working to clean up the air and water.

So, when we read about pollution, we should not be too discouraged. We should remember that a start has been made, and the progress will continue. Science will help, but so must we.

Now that we have come to the end of this book, you know that science means taking time to wonder, to ask "Why?" "Why is the sky blue?" "Why do winds blow?"

Science will lead you to ask questions. Sometimes you may find answers, but for some questions, such as, "What is the inside of the moon made of?" "What is electricity?" there are no known answers yet.

Test! Test! Test! That is the way the scientist tries to find new truths.

Index

Anaconda, Montana, and pollution, 59
anthropology, 28
Apollo, 50
astronauts, experiences of, 55-57
astronomy, 8, 21
atoms, 20

Ben Franklin, 52
biology, 23
blackout, in New York City, 12-13
bob, experiments with, 33-38
Borman, Frank, 56-57
botany, 23

chemistry, 20, 29
coal, things made from, 9
Collins, Michael, 55-56
curiosity, and science, 14-18, 29

data-gatherers, 46-48
detective, scientist as, 29

Eagle, 18
Earth, astronauts and, 56-57
earth sciences, splitting of, 29
economics, 27
Einstein, Albert, 50
electricity, 11-13, 50, 51
experimentation, *see* experiments
experiments, 30, 31-46

Galilei, Galileo, experiments of, 31-43, 48

geology, 22, 29
glass, from sand, 7-8
Grand Canyon, 22
Gulf Stream, voyage in, 52-53

Hale telescope, 15
hydrogen, 20

inclined plane, 39-40

laser, ruby red, 48
life sciences, 19, 23-25
London, and pollution, 59-61
Los Angeles, and pollution, 58

Mariana Trench, 16
mathematics, and science, 46
Meister, Joseph, 45-46
Missoula, Montana, and pollution, 58
molecules, 20
moon, flights to, 18, 50; mystery of, 51

National Wildlife Federation, quote from booklet of, 11
Nautilus, 14-15
Newton, Sir Isaac, 50, 54
New York City, blackout in, 12-13; and pollution, 58
North Pole, 14
nuclear power, 50

observation, 31
oxygen, 20, 24, 43

paleontology, 25

Palomar Observatory, 15
Pasteur, Louis, 23, 43-46
pendulum, 33-38
Phoenix, Arizona, and
    pollution, 58
physical sciences, 19-22
physics, 19
physiology, 24
Piccard, Jacques, 16-17, 52-53
Pisa, Cathedral of, 31;
    Leaning Tower of, 40
plants, and oxygen, 43
Polar Ice Cap, 14
political science, 26
pollution, water and air, 11, 57-61
Priestley, Joseph, 43

rabies, 44-46
revelations, 50
rivers, pollution of, 11
rocks, from moon, 51

San Bernardino National Forest, 58
sand, and glass, 7-8
science, things achieved by, 5-12, 55;
  what it is, 14-30;
  different methods of, 46-50;

problems and mysteries of, 51, 53, 54;
and future, 55-62;
see also scientists
scientific method, 40, 43-49
scientists, things achieved by, 5-12, 55;
and curiosity, 14-18, 29;
as detectives, 29;
see also science
Sioux Indians, 28
social science, 26
social sciences, 19, 26-28
submarines, 14, 16

telescopes, 8, 15
theory makers, 46, 48, 50
Townes, Dr. Charles, 48, 50
Trieste, 16

vaccine, for rabies, 45-46

water, clean, and science, 10-11;
  see also pollution
weights, experiments with, 33-36, 38-40

x-ray machines, 15